I Love

Baby Animals

By Steve Parker
Illustrated by Ian Jackson

First published in 2006 by
Miles Kelly Publishing Ltd
Bardfield Centre, Great Bardfield, Essex, CM7 4SL

Copyright © Miles Kelly Publishing Ltd 2006

2 4 6 8 10 9 7 5 3 1

Editorial Director Belinda Gallagher
Art Director Jo Brewer
Junior Designer Candice Bekir
Cover Artworker Stephan Davis
Production Manager Elizabeth Brunwin
Reprographics Stephan Davis

ISBN 1-84236-781-1

Printed in China

British Library Cataloguing-in-Publication Data
A catalogue record for this book is available
from the British Library

www.mileskelly.net
info@mileskelly.net

Contents

Giant panda cub

A newborn giant panda cub is smaller than your hand. It is white all over, has almost no fur, and its eyes are tightly closed. The cub grows quickly. By six weeks old it can leave its den and follow its mother. By six months old it is eating its favourite food – bamboo.

The baby panda is born in a den, a cave or a hollow tree. The mother leaves it twice a day to look for food and water.

4

The female panda usually gives birth to just one cub, but sometimes she has two. She may have as many as eight cubs in her lifetime.

Panda face!
Make a panda face from white card, with four black circles. Can people guess what you are?

When a baby panda is hungry, it will cry like a human baby. The cub stays with its mother for over a year.

Grey wolf cubs

For the first few weeks of their lives, grey wolf cubs stay inside their den, cave or burrow. **Their mother feeds them on milk.** Then they begin to leave the den and start to eat meat.

The cubs nip, pounce, and tumble. This is practice for when they grow up to hunt their own food.

The mother wolf usually has three to five cubs. Sometimes she may have as many as ten!

Wolf cubs are brought their first meaty meals not only by their mother, but by their father too – and by other members of the wolf pack.

Howling wolf

Wolves do not really howl at the Moon. They are simply telling other wolves 'I'm here!'

Penguin chick

No baby animal grows up in a colder place than the emperor penguin chick. It is -50 degrees Celsius in icy Antarctica, colder than a food deep freezer. Luckily the chick has its father to keep it warm.

Who's taller?

The emperor penguin is the biggest penguin. It is 120 centimetres in height. How tall are you?

Father penguins shelter younger chicks in their belly feathers.

The penguin chick cheeps and pecks its father's beak. This makes the parent bring up food from its stomach for the chick to eat.

After two months at sea catching food, the mother penguin returns to her baby. Now the father can go off to feed.

Older chicks grow fluffy feathers. They huddle together for extra warmth in the icy wind.

Elephant calf

A baby elephant has the world's biggest, strongest family to look after it. Not only does it have its mother, but also older sisters, aunties, and even its grandmother, who leads the whole herd.

The mother constantly touches her baby with her trunk. If she is busy feeding, an older sister or aunt 'babysits' and keeps the calf out of danger.

Cool, mum!

When a baby elephant wants to rest, its mother stands so that her shadow keeps the baby shaded and cool.

For the first year or two, the calf stays close to its mother.

The baby feeds on its mother's milk for up to four years.

A young male elephant leaves the main herd when he is about 12 years old. He joins other young males to make a smaller herd.

Orang-utan baby

A baby orang-utan is like a human baby, except hairier! It sleeps a lot, cries when it is hungry or frightened, and goes to the toilet where it wants. The mother orang-utan is very caring and protects her baby from enemies, such as large eagles.

A baby orang-utan may stay with its mother for as long as eight years.

As the young orang-utan grows, it begins to try different foods. It will eat mainly fruits, flowers and buds.

Orang-utans live in trees. They are good climbers. Their feet and toes grasp almost as well as their hands and fingers.

Great ape!
The male orang-utan is twice as big as the female. At 80 kilograms, he is the world's heaviest tree-living creature.

The young orang-utan feeds on its mother's milk for three years or more.

Fawn

A baby deer is called a fawn. Its coat is covered in white spots. As the sun shines through leaves and twigs, it makes light spots on the woodland floor – just like the spots on a fawn's coat. The fawn lies still and silent. Its mother stays nearby, feeding and watching.

The white, spotty coat blends in with patches of sunlight on the ground. This makes the fawn difficult to see.

Big head!

A buck is a fully grown male deer. He grows huge antlers each summer. They fall off in late winter.

The fawn has huge ears, big eyes and a good sense of smell. If an enemy comes too near, the fawn jumps up and runs away.

The doe (mother deer) visits her baby to feed it on her milk. Then she goes back to the herd.

Kittens

A mother cat is very busy. She has to feed her kittens, keep them warm, lick them clean, let them climb all over her and stop them wandering into danger. She may have ten or more kittens to care for.

A kitten learns to crawl first. By about four weeks old it can walk. A week later it is running and jumping.

Popular pets

Some years ago, dogs were the most popular pets. Now cats have taken over. How many pet cats do you know?

Kittens can recognize each other by smell, even in total darkness.

A kitten feeds on its mother's milk for about eight weeks. It begins to eat other foods at three weeks.

17

Joey

A baby kangaroo is called a joey. For the first six months of its life, it lives in its mother's pocket-shaped pouch. Here it is safe, feeding on her milk. Soon, the joey grows strong enough to leave the pouch and explore. If danger appears, it hops back in again.

A young joey is very shy. It rushes back to the pouch every minute. Soon it becomes braver and stays out of the pouch longer.

The older joey still pops its head into its mother's pouch to feed on her milk until it is almost a year old.

The mother kangaroo has to clean her pouch often, using her paws, teeth and tongue. She throws out bits of dirt and fur that her joey leaves behind – and its droppings too!

Hop hop hop
Can you hop like a kangaroo? Keep your feet together, knees bent, and hands held up like paws.

When the joey is eight months old it leaves the pouch and never comes back. It still stays near its mother.

19

Baby otters

Many baby animals like to play – especially otter babies! They roll, tumble and jump in the riverbank mud. Sometimes they have pretend fights. This play is practice for when the otters have to hunt their own food.

Lazy otters

After a big meal, an otter spends a day or two lazing on a bare patch of ground, called its 'couch' or 'sofa'.

The otters stay in their burrow for two months. Then their mother leads them out to the riverbank, where they play and learn to swim.

By the time otters are four months old they can catch fish, baby frogs and waterbird chicks.

The baby otters grow a thick, waterproof coat that keeps them warm and dry in the water.

Seal pup

The harp seal pup lives in the Arctic. This baby is surrounded by snow, ice and freezing cold sea – as well as hungry hunters such as polar bears and wolves. The pup lies perfectly still. Its thick, white fur keeps it warm and hides it in its snowy surroundings.

If a pup cannot find its mother, it wails and cries like a human baby.

Harp seals eat mainly fish such as herring, cod and capelin. They might try a snack of squid.